CONTENTS

THE EXPONENTIAL UNIVERSE

FOREWORD

This book deep dives head-first into sensitive topics which I believe to be among the most important to exist.

Everything written is my own view, but I have tried to draw conclusions which are logical, impartial, well researched, thought out and self-evident.
I have done my best to gather the most substantiated facts and theories that I could find.

I am sure that I have failed on all those counts but I can honestly say that I have scoured my mind with wire wool and wrestled with the concepts like some kind of crazed cage fighter – sometimes for many years before reaching any kind of conclusive results.

I have had to do 180-degree turns more times than a merry-go-round and I have also gone all round the houses only to eventually come full circle on more occasions than I can count and I know that it is going to happen again and again for the foreseeable future.

The skills that we have today will never be enough for the jobs of tomorrow, but we are all in it together.
Whether we like it or not.

CHAPTER 1 : OUR PART IN THE PLAY

Nothing that Newton, Da Vinci or Einstein did was ever enough.
The same applies to Jesus, Muhammad and Buddha !
Nothing that me or you ever achieves will be enough.

You will never be enough for your wife / husband / partner and he / she will never be enough for you.
BUT
All together we **are** actually more than anyone will ever need.

That means every animal, insect, plant and substance that exists – down to the smallest blade of grass, grain of sand or gentle caress of a summer's breeze.

We are here to be designers, inventors, creators, master artisans, guardians, adventurers, explorers…..

We are not tools or machines.

You are not a driver, baker, builder, doctor, astrophysicist.

You are a human being who drives, bakes, builds, heals and studies the stars.

"Our imagination is stretched to the utmost, not, as in fiction, to imagine things that are not really there, but just to comprehend those things which ARE there."

– Richard Feynman

From one perspective, this life is like a big, eternal test.

But we all fail and we always will, largely because we're trying to prove that our particular version of truth is the right one ALREADY.

We are **already** correct about exactly NOTHING.
As a baby we start out knowing zero and we are now correct about a small number of things that we have learned during our lifetime.

For anyone to assume that they should constantly be right in a universe of this size, age and complexity, it is so excruciatingly mindless that, in total fairness, they should be culled for stupidity!
Mwahahaaa !!!

It is our responsibility to find out how we fit into society – not the other way round.

Every other creature and thing combined is so much more important than our tiny body.
There is only one of us, but there are **trillions** of other people and creatures.

Every life form maintains our existence – from the roads, houses, vehicles, furniture and warmth to exquisite delicacies more plentiful than anyone will ever count to breath-taking vistas and landscapes of beauty beyond compare…

Not to mention the innumerable masterpiece symphonies and works of wonder which fill our auditory, olfactory, visual and tactile senses with more 'perfection' than we will ever be able to scratch the surface of.

Everyone starts out life with no particular purpose.
We all decide on our own reasons to be here.

By the time a child reaches adulthood, they have taken almost everything FOR FREE over their whole life.
The least we can do is try our best to give something back while we

take more from this place than we will EVER be able to repay.

As you grow up, you become more and more capable. (exceptions apply e.g.: severely injured)
The more capable you become, the more you will be expected to contribute.
If you decide to ignore your responsibilities, don't be surprised when you aren't appreciated.
Respect has to be built over years because proven statistical evidence is very telling.

All adult humans with healthy bodies have the ability to contribute more than they take from this World.
If you take more than you give back then you are called a parasite.

People who do not currently have a positive, measurable contribution to society had better start to think of how they can help the key workers.

If you cannot think of ONE single thing that you can do to help ONE single other suffering soul on this dying planet that we're all desperately trying to survive on then you are clearly one of the monsters.

Do you think that it is hard to make a living if you are honest ?
Do you think that you have to lie to get ahead in business ?
Or cheat ?
Or maybe steal ?
Or, should you be as mean and miserly as possible ?
Surely that will make you rich ?

Is it such a difficult idea to understand, that we should only ever expect to get what we rightfully earn ?

Finding love for doing what we enjoy is the easy part but most people end up ignoring passions which are more important – the things we hate – and their repair.
It is so much easier to just leave it to somebody else, right ?

As far as I can tell, since WWII the societies of most nations have only become more and more dependent and weak as time has gone by.

The decadent ways of the west have created masses of people who treat their bodies like sewage pipes or crash test dummies – pumping themselves full of whatever revolting concoction that the local brewery, drugstore or butcher has just dragged in.

We might live longer but it isn't exactly worth it if you are on a life support machine or guzzling pills just to get through the day or suffering from a nasty ailment or affliction – of which there is such a wide and varied assortment to choose from !

It seems to me that almost every person and every society throws out a lot of babies with a lot of bathwater in terms of the evolutionary advancements that children do not learn from their parents – losing more knowledge and wisdom than anyone will ever know over the course of history.

Nothing that you ever do is going to repay our ancestors for undergoing the indescribable trials and terrors which have dragged us further from chaos.

We may not be able to repay those who have given their lives for us over the course of history but there are those who are **currently** giving up most pleasures every single day – consigning themselves to a life of constant risk – protecting and saving others, facing criminals, healing infectious people, building our world, teaching our children and so much more than I can scribble with a few paltry words, including sacrifices that make everyone else look like weak-minded, useless, cowards.

The few carry the many.
But it just isn't really possible.

Our ancestors did not have the hindsight and experience that we have today – being the benefactors of the monumental achievements of all those who have come before us.

By and large, they were more ignorant – as it can only be when you look back in history – but they had courage and determination.

We are standing on the shoulders of giants.

CHAPTER 2 : EXPONENTIAL IGNORANCE

Our cosmos is hurtling in every direction at around 300,000 kilometres per second.
We come from infinity and we're heading for eternity.
An epic scale is the order of the day.

As the Universe gets bigger, "know-it-alls" become more frustrated, stupid and glaringly obvious.

Everyone lives in their own little 'tunnel' of understanding which only extends as far as our current knowledge, experience and wisdom allows.
It is a very short, narrow, irrational view which is more selfish and less ethical than anyone realises.

The vast majority of the conclusions that we have drawn in our lifetime are based on one-off wonders, other people's opinions, unverified facts, bias, illogical emotions, and blind assumptions as far as the eye can see.

Variables are also increasing and changing exponentially.

The world often looks like a very random place until one understands some of the principles and patterns which are followed by each of the anomalous or chaotic looking phenomena that we observe throughout our life.
People call it chance when they do not understand the principles in play.

Everyone everywhere is exponentially ignorant and always will be.

If it were within the most distant and vague realms of plausibility to measure the amount of reality that we know, including all of history, the fraction would be less than 0.1% of 0.1% of 0.1% of 0.1% .....e

However unimaginably small the number is (and not one person could ever calculate it) the percentage that we are currently aware of shrinks with every second of every day.

More and more people experiencing more and more, discovering more and more, composing more and more, inventing more and more, creating more and more... in faster and better ways all the time.
Most of us, anyway.

As an entire species, we know next to absolute zero about every aspect of every one of the most elementary particles and their interactions – between the dawn of time and today.

Mostly, people are ignorant, primitive and incapable because they have not had the time to learn yet, but some of the strongest, most intelligent, formidable individuals have been working so hard at avoiding responsibility for so long and with such dedication that they are not really much good at anything else.

Skills that enable production, maintenance and development are needed if you want to evolve and improve your life.
Inventing excuses, fabricating tales, disinformation and lies, evading blame, manipulating others, cheating and profiteering are not talents of any real substance or value.

One big problem with the vast majority of the unscientifically educated general public is that they desperately desire certainty in areas where it does not exist.
That means most places.

In fairness, there is not a single scientist or human who can say that there is no area in which they are searching for certainty where it does not exist.

That will never be possible because **everything** is uncertain until we have had a chance to explore it.

That said, truly educated, experienced, wise people have a much better idea of how much there IS to know, among other things.
If we don't know about the options that are available to us then it is extremely unlikely that we will be able to take advantage of them.

The more educated that we become, the more we should realise how much more there **is** to know and that it is NEVER going to be possible for ANYBODY to have the blind certainty that so many brain-dead narcissists are pretending to have already.
They can only fool other idiots mostly.

We can't just make it all up as we go along.
Nobody knows who or what we are, how we got here or why we do... anything at all, but everybody takes offense when anybody dares to imply that they don't know how life or the world works !

If our gaze ventures a bit further than our nose, we should never assume that anyone should know anything.
If our little mind were to suddenly grasp a trillion, trillion, trillionth of the true age, size or power of this place it would go pop – all across the Universe.

The more we learn, the more we realise how small, insignificant, ineffectual, inadequate and utterly overpowered we are.
If you're doing it right, that is.

In a macrocosm that is more ancient and intricate than anybody will ever know, it becomes more and more impossible to prove that you know enough.
About ANY subject.

We need to adopt the attitude of a child to discover HOW things work, as opposed to hopelessly trying to prove that impulsive, assumptive, shallow, self-centred, blinkered theories are already right.

If you are always trying to prove that you are right about every-thing then you are GUARANTEED to fail **every - single - day**.
We need to take those same theories and find out if they are true or NOT !

And since they were probably sucked straight out of our thumb or based on something that we heard in a movie or down the pub the other night, I suggest that we get ready to be WRONG.
Again and again and again.....e

Even grand, thought-out, comprehensive scientific theories are mostly wrong.
As in over 99 %.

In a big wide World, where the most learned people of all time know little-to-nothing, boundless megalomaniacal oblivious arrogance is more obvious by the day.
Stop trying to pretend that you understand this existence better than a wide-eyed child.

CHAPTER 3 : EVOLUTIONARY SHORTCUTS

If we get over ourself enough to learn the good habits of everyone else, we can skip many centuries of evolution – rather than desperately trying to figure out **all** of our problems **all** by ourself.

We can conceptually 'copy' every useful habit from every other being without becoming a plagiarist or losing our identity.

We all change behaviour continually, so if we make the conscious decision to learn the best skills and habits from any of the countless geniuses, gurus and heroes of our World then we become more and more unique because we always approach, analyse and do things in our own style anyway – which is already more original than anyone can possibly comprehend.

No-one else thinks like you.

What's more difficult is realising that the people who we see as stupid, crazy, nasty, sick or twisted also have things to teach us which are vital for our survival – and don't worry – you don't have to learn anybody's nasty habits.
Just the ones you choose.

Don't write-off every single one of a scumbag's ideas and don't believe every single word that masters tell you.

We should never dismiss a single thing without due consideration.
But we can logically eliminate.

We need to be open to learning anything at any time from anyone. Some of the greatest insights can come from some of the most unlikely places.

Whether anyone admits it or not, we all search for faults in everyone around us, and we **always** find them – often where they don't even exist – possibly making us feel superior for a moment, but we seldom search for our own faults.

Instead, we have a rose-tinted view of ourself and maybe a few close friends or family to some extent.
How many people are stricter on themselves than they are on others ?
It is difficult though.

We need to see someone behaving worse than us first before we are able to accept that we have the same / similar problem.
Until then we just can't face our failures.

So, slag everybody off to death every day but **do it in your head**, be specific and then think about whether you are being too harsh or not.
Analyse the issue thoroughly and revisit it on a different day.

Be very sure when making accusations.
Never blurt them out.
Or get ready for embarrassment, ridicule, frustration, anger and violence.

If we feel that we are 'last in the race' or the only one with a particular shortcoming then our mind just refuses to accept a whole bunch of facts which prove that we're incorrect in some way – which means that we NEVER resolve the issue.

So many of our truly powerful mental skills, like investigation, analysis and judgment are continually wasted on ranting about news, media, government, Armageddon, conspiracies, revolution, pollution, sport...

I'm not saying that we should ignore these things – in fact they need to be studied systematically but if we get too hung up on any of them individually, we become more and more blinkered and unable to see the bigger picture.

We should only regularly worry about things that we can affect. So, complaining about the government is COMPLETELY pointless – unless you can do something constructive to help the situation. If not, keep your mouth shut.

We all want to be successful at everything we do, but most of us are not willing to put in the groundwork or accept our failings... which is okay if you want to guarantee defeat before you start.

When we accept our weaknesses, we can turn them into strengths.
It is a strange paradox – to learn a subject, we have to first admit our ignorance of it.
If you pretend that there is no hole in your armour then you won't fix it.

As long as a person is searching for ways to "be right" all the time, they will miss the point and usually the truth.
We need to search for what "is right", while being able to accept the facts that go against whatever it is that we're trying to prove.

If we do not learn to do this, we will keep going around the maze of life with hardly any real knowledge in our head – just a bunch of ideas that seemed good and suited us at the time.

We need to use the investigation, analysis and judgment that we already have on ourselves. For a start, because we are almost always the only one who we CAN truly judge.

Removal of superstition, corruption of all kinds and irrational assumptions are necessary if we are ever going to get a true view of what is going on around us.

But nobody knows where our superstition, corruption and as-

sumptions begin...
Or end.

It's not an easy place to figure stuff out, this Universe.
The rules of the game seem to have changed more times than I think anyone will ever know.

From quarks to protons to atoms to molecules to single-celled organisms to complex plant, insect and animal structures.....

Each of the above lives on a different level of existence, in a way. You might even say a different dimension – with systems, principles and even physical laws that can be so ridiculously different that they often seem alien.

Everyone has divine talents and everyone has infernal faults. Recognition and acceptance of both is absolutely necessary for our progression.

Sometimes others are here to teach us **what** to do and other times they are here to teach us what **not** to do.

Sometimes you will think that a person's good habit is a bad habit and sometimes you will think that a person's bad habit is a good habit.

We have to figure out what is right and what is wrong in every situation.

Understanding is a never ending and messy process – very slowly becoming less and less vague and confusing as you progress – until one day it begins to get clearer and clearer in **some** areas – when you desire truth like your life depends on it.

It does.

The rehabilitation of our mind is like repairing a broken machine with a broken tool and no manual or training or knowledge of how the machine should work or even what it is.

You are here to change my way of thinking and I am here to change

your way of thinking.
But truth and facts don't care about our opinions…
Unless they are based on truth and facts.

Our version of good and correct is not always good and correct.
Our version of truth and justice is not always truth and justice.

Our version of reality is a fictional fairy-tale, the foundations of which are based ENTIRELY on blind assumptions.

THERE ARE NO EXCEPTIONS.

Most of us seem to want lots of things lots of ways :

To learn less and less but know more and more…
To do less and less but get more and more…
To give respect less and less but receive more and more…

Rather than just trying to do less and less, try to ACCOMPLISH more and more with less and less energy.
That's the best deal you're ever going to get.

No matter how many records there are or how many times we break them, someone will always come along and go one better.
No matter how advanced anything ever gets, it will eventually be improved upon.

I believe that information, expansion and evolution are all exponential.

If you have not decided to learn more and more then the world will pass you by and leave you behind.

CHAPTER 4 : PRIORITY SCIENCE

In 2010 I began to obsess with the question "What is the best thing that I can learn or do right now that will progress my career / life forward the quickest and easiest."

It is just so hard to figure out what it is that we don't know, but should know or would benefit most from.

There is no final answer to that question and there never will be.

We need the habit of asking ourself "what is the best course of action from this point onwards" because 'this point' is an ever-changing thing.

We need two opposing character traits – the determination to follow through to the bitter end like a bulldog with a bone and also the flexibility to make a U-turn when we realise that our path is doomed to failure even when that means a complete overhaul at the last minute.

The subjects of study and aspects of our psyche that we need to face are the ones that we currently avoid at all costs.

Inner demons, cognitive dissonance and irrational assumptions are a very common part of every 'non-insane' person.

If we ignore our hang-ups, they will eventually be our undoing.

If we face the music and grab the bullshit by the horns, we can turn our flaws into assets by focusing on the chinks in our armour

and doing something about them.
If we ignore them as much as possible, they worsen as much as possible.

Dealing with our biggest problems is not fun in the moment but it enables the greatest possible leaps in progression because we gain benefits but also lose the nastiest, most rotten, distorted effects from our lives and ourselves which are the things that hold us back the most.

We have to search for ALL of the reasons that EVERYTHING is our fault as opposed to hurling wild accusations based on instant judgments, fickle and biased emotions, sectarian dogmas, anecdotal data and irrational assumptions without any attempt at logical, systematic research or analysis.

In our own lives, a huge amount of our problems ARE our fault anyway.

If we confront and accept our limitations, we can chip them away. We can also begin to discover and assess our real strengths – with reason.
It is surprising how many of our greatest skills that we take for granted because we have been doing them for such a long time.

Another benefit is that we will begin to stop trying to live up to so many unrealistic expectations and attempting things that are impossible which will enable us to release some of the weight of the World from our shoulders.

Eventually we may even start to accept the limitations of others and then one day maybe we will stop expecting so much from them.

You are not alone with the guilty, embarrassed, ashamed feelings that you face. We're all inadequate losers together !

We do have a wide range of diverse problems and many are similar or even identical but every one of us is 100 % custom-screwed.

CHAPTER 5 : THE 'VIRTUAL' WAR

This is the most unique disaster ever.

We are slap-bang in the middle of a **sustained** worldwide cataclysm, as in a world war, yet we are still here with the ability to analyse the details while we are still in it and even have endless varied discussions about its myriad aspects while we're at it.

Not to mention all of the songs, tributes, articles, bulletins, conferences, committees, task forces, advisory groups like SAGE and more than I could list if I were here for the rest of the week.

We have no major disruptions to our supply chains for food, medicine and necessities. We have a government that actually listens and responds to scientists and journalists.

I know that they are all far from perfect, but they do a hell of a lot more than the whinging, over expectant, thankless moaners of this world who just add to the problem, offering ZERO help while criticizing the people who are desperately struggling to dig us out of our hell-hole.

We have teams of news professionals who track down truth to the bitter end every single day, as do our amazing philosophers and scientists.

We have police, army, navy, air force, border patrols, prison and fire officers, care and emergency services who protect, heal and care for us EVERY SECOND OF EVERY DAY OF EVERY WEEK OF

EVERY MONTH OF EVERY YEAR.

For the vast majority, the greatest reward that the true heroes of our world will ever receive is a pat on the back and a few words – no matter how many lives they save or how much physical and mental trauma that they endure or how many REAL sacrifices that they make – even if they spend their **entire** life helping others.

When a person has to watch people die in their arms on a regular basis, their mind has to find some way to develop a coping mechanism.

This will almost certainly involve a 'switching off' of some of the emotional responses to deaths or death statistics, for example – which is absolutely necessary in order to perform structured, logical analyses, draw clear conclusions and take decisive actions.

So next time you sit in your armchair issuing rampant expectations, rhetoric and hypocritical attacks – remember how much **you** do and that they would come apart at the seams emotionally and physically if they were to allow themselves to dwell for very long on the death of every single person.

More is going to be learned from the experiences to come than by any other in history.
Collectively, humanity has the greatest understanding and ability that we have ever had and all the time in the world to apply them.

Before Covid-19, at times I had hoped for some kind of event that would unite us toward a common purpose like an alien invasion or something.
This virus could be just what the doctor ordered !

Carbon emissions have been drastically reduced, societies are accelerating the rate of progression toward a digital life including remote working which will reduce the need for physical media, travel and overall time while increasing the potential for enhanced productivity and service standards.

I see people helping each other, companies and armies repurposing resources for vital services, science beginning to take a more prominent role in making the decisions that govern our lives.
I also like that people are starting to think a bit more about what is really important in life.

We, the British Nation, are the central pillar for truth and justice in this World.

We hold the mother of parliaments, the father of police forces, the first fire brigade and free National Health Service.

Our laws are in drastic need of an overhaul but as far as I can tell we have the most fair, equal and ethical ones that have ever existed.

People in this country take so many things for granted.
A shocking amount.

Prime minister's questions, daily press briefings where ministers and top government officials actually answer questions – maybe not all of them – but I believe that it is fair to say that they are drilled more relentlessly than any other parliament.

Our news reporters enjoy some of the greatest freedoms of any on this planet, yet the government stands up to their scrutiny quite well.

I know that you probably don't agree but when you have the most transparent parliamentary system on Earth, it is very easy to find faults with it.
There will always be problems in life.

It is not the government's fault that they aren't **all** fixed.

CHAPTER 6 : ACTIONS HAVE CONSEQUENCES

The world works by cause and effect.
However hard anyone might try to disprove it, NOBODY is above the law.

Some people have been getting away with crimes of all kinds for so long that it is habitual for them. A way of life.

I want to see all parasites, profiteers, dictators and true criminals of every kind eradicated from our world.

No cuddling, no indulgence – like children, prisoners must understand that what they did was wrong, why it was wrong and that it is unacceptable to do it again.

Hugs and kisses do not rehabilitate violent offenders.

They need to receive some of their own punishment if they are not very contrite – like being stolen from if they are a thief.
'Own medicine therapy', I call it.

Some very innovative programs can be developed by some top psychiatrists, health and probation service professionals.

Remember – a criminal is stripped of some fundamental human rights when they are incarcerated.
They have made an attack on EVERY INNOCENT PERSON and must be in a system that causes them to be truly rehabilitated.

One of the biggest problems is that no one feels the pain of others.

To remedy this, criminals need to feel the effects of their 'causes' or actions.
Until they understand the pain that they inflict, they must experience it.

Until such a time they must be separated from the rest of society because children and other vulnerable people have a right to walk the streets without fear of loss, harm and death.

If you take another human life, you owe your own and have no chance for true rehabilitation.
Not in this life.

Also, you cannot really save ONE other person – you can only learn to save yourself a bit better and help others to learn how to save themselves a bit better...

Do you want to nurture a rapist who may rape you and your family or a policeman who would protect your life with theirs... or a nurse who would care for you every single day whenever needed ?

If you are kind to the cruel, you oppress the kind.
If you allow bad behaviour, you will get more of it.

The NHS, care, police, emergency services, the legal profession, prison service, government and all key workers are among the most under-appreciated people in our world.

BUT WE NEED THEM THE MOST !!!

CHAPTER 7 : PERIPHERAL ECONOMY

Half* of society has to work about ten* times harder because the other half* refuses to grow a spine, a conscience, clean up their mess, take responsibility for their actions, help someone besides themselves or stop killing things on a whim.

* I don't know the exact figures but I know that they are much too high.

We are learning about EXACTLY which jobs, organisations and people are needed in this world.

Kiddies' playground games like the premier league, "professional" sport and the entire gambling industry have ZERO contribution to the improvement and development of our society.

Or any society.

They drain vast amounts of resources and are role models for the perversion and deterioration of morality, progress and all true civilisation.

Don't get me wrong – I see sport and entertainment as a healthy part of a natural, varied lifestyle but when you devote your entire life to them you become a pathetic narcissist with a distorted sense of priorities who is just really good at kicking a ball around, for example.

Some of the fittest and most capable people that exist are squandering their abilities on fiddling while Rome is burning.

I am not referring to the current pandemic.
This has been the case for centuries at least.

I believe that the Corona Virus is the best thing that has happened to our economy in a long time.

The inclusion of revenues generated by sport and betting into GDP statistics give an over-inflated picture of a countries' economy as they provide nothing functional or tangible.

You will have to get your jollies some other way.
Like playing with your plonker.
At least you can feel happy in the knowledge that you will have the same contribution as someone who is playing with balls.

The beliefs, principles, morals and desires of the vast majority have created an environment which has detached true value from things – allowing bloodsuckers to be paid fortunes for debauched depravity, twiddling their willies, decimating the planet and devouring all life in their path while our real saviours are exploited to breaking-point by being expected to DEVOTE their lives to untold risk for pathetic wages and if they don't then they are guilted into oblivion with public / patient health, safety, needs, Hippocratic oaths and many other things.

Some people never plan to be any help to ANYONE ANYWHERE.
Many plan to do quite the opposite.

In my experience, most people think that every creature is here to lay down its life for them to violate, molest, plunder, chew up and spit out just for kicks, giggles and cheap thrills.

If you think that ANY BODY is here to kill itself just for your pleasure then YOU are the one who deserves to be obliterated.

When some people die, it is a great loss to the world.
When other people die, the world is a better place because of it.

What do YOU do to improve anyone else's life?

Why would anybody want you around?

If you don't have detailed, specific examples (otherwise known as ACTUAL examples) then there is literally no reason for you to be here and we will all forget you quickly when you're gone.

Almost everybody has abandoned the true order of priority and command in this world.
Food, shelter, health and security are at the top of this list.
I love music and the arts but they are not necessary for our survival.
Why don't you tell a starving Syrian refugee child how important your entertainment is.

At the end of it all we are going to learn how little work that there is to do – when the monsters, parasites and cancers are eradicated and everybody left over is helping to pick up the pieces of our predicament and mucking-in with ALL of the worst jobs.

Dealing with heinous criminals, dying people, fires, other emergencies, hazardous waste, chemicals, extreme environments of all kinds, dangers of every variety, immense trials of fortitude, patience and determination – are all examples of what ALL of the spoiled shirkers of the world are going to be helping with.

Printed in Great Britain
by Amazon

61769955R00019